Truck Driver Tom

MONICA
WELLINGTON

Dutton
Children's
Books

The artwork was prepared from color copies of photos cut and pasted onto paper painted with gouache.

DUTTON CHILDREN'S BOOKS
A division of Penguin Young Readers Group

Published by the Penguin Group
Penguin Group (USA) Inc., 375 Hudson Street, New York,
New York 10014, U.S.A. • Penguin Group (Canada), 90 Eglinton
Avenue East, Suite 700, Toronto, Ontario, Canada M4P 2Y3
(a division of Pearson Penguin Canada Inc.) • Penguin Books
Ltd, 80 Strand, London WC2R 0RL, England • Penguin Ireland,
25 St Stephen's Green, Dublin 2, Ireland (a division of Penguin
Books Ltd) • Penguin Group (Australia), 250 Camberwell Road,
Camberwell, Victoria 3124, Australia (a division of Pearson
Australia Group Pty Ltd) • Penguin Books India Pvt Ltd,
11 Community Centre, Panchsheel Park, New Delhi - 110 017,
India • Penguin Group (NZ), 67 Apollo Drive, Rosedale, North
Shore 0745, Auckland, New Zealand (a division of Pearson
New Zealand Ltd) • Penguin Books (South Africa) (Pty) Ltd, 24
Sturdee Avenue, Rosebank, Johannesburg 2196, South Africa
Penguin Books Ltd, Registered Offices: 80 Strand,
London WC2R 0RL, England

Library of Congress Cataloging-in-Publication Data

Wellington, Monica.
Truck driver Tom / Monica Wellington.—1st ed.   p. cm.
Summary: The driver of a tractor-trailer picks up a load of
fresh fruits and vegetables, then drives through the country-
side, past small towns, and into the big city, passing farms,
construction sites, and many other vehicles, then delivers
the produce and relaxes with other drivers.
ISBN 978-0-525-47831-7 (hardcover)
[1. Truck drivers—Fiction. 2. Tractor-trailers—Fiction.
3. Transportation—Fiction.] I. Title.
PZ7.W4576Tru 2007   [E]—dc22   2006035911

Published in the United States by
Dutton Children's Books,
a division of Penguin Young Readers Group
345 Hudson Street, New York, New York 10014
www.penguin.com/youngreaders

Designed by Abby Kuperstock
Manufactured in China • First Edition
1 3 5 7 9 10 8 6 4 2

To Jack and Kelly

Tom loves to drive his big truck. **VROOM, VROOM.** He revs up his engine. He is off to pick up his load.

The farmers have a lot of fresh fruits and vegetables ready for him. **"LOOKING GOOD."** Tom keeps track of the order as they haul it onto his truck.

CLANK, CLANK.

Farm trucks are working in the fields. Tom blasts his horn to them. He is on his way.

He has miles and miles ahead to drive.

ZOOM, ZOOM. He roars down the highway.

Up he goes over the mountain,

down into the valley, and **WHOOSH**, into the tunnel.

"DELAYS AHEAD!" squawks the CB radio.

Tom slows down for road construction.

Tom needs to stretch his legs.
He stops for snacks and gas.
"FILL 'ER UP." He is making
good progress on his trip across
the country to the city.

But Tom has to take a detour. **BUMPITY BUMP.**

He loses time with all the traffic in the village.

People head to the city—by boat, plane, train, car.

RUMBLE, RUMBLE. Tom crosses the bridge.

BEEP, BEEP.

HONK, HONK.

Tom arrives in
the big city at last.
Buildings are rising,
and streets are
crowded.

Tom delivers his load of
fresh fruits and vegetables.
CHECK, CHECK.

The order is complete.

His job is done, well done.

Tom is hungry, and he finally has time to relax. **"WHAT'LL IT BE?"** asks the waitress. He meets many trucker friends at his favorite diner.

Tomorrow he will hit the road with new cargo on a new route. But now it's time to sleep in his cozy nook. At the truck stop, big trucks hum. Good night, Tom.

"OVER AND OUT."

Tom's 18-wheeler truck

Can you find all these **TRUCKS** and **VEHICLES** in the book?

bicycle

pickup truck

tractor with plow

tractor with hopper

milk truck

combine

horse trailer and farm truck

tractor with grapple

hay gatherer

dinosaur delivery truck

tractor

flatbed truck with house

transport truck

double-trailer truck

motor home

convertible

tank truck

limousine

log carrier

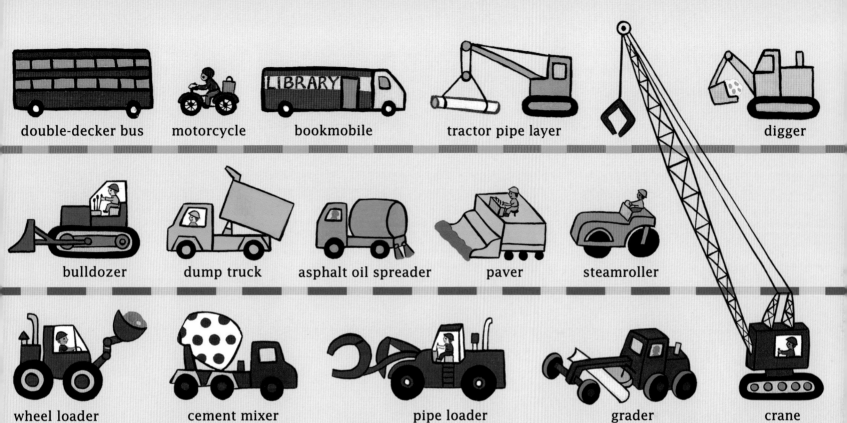

double-decker bus · motorcycle · bookmobile · tractor pipe layer · digger

bulldozer · dump truck · asphalt oil spreader · paver · steamroller

wheel loader · cement mixer · pipe loader · grader · crane

mail truck

piano van

moving van

taxi

ice-cream truck

tow truck

garbage truck

ambulance

fire engine

police car

street sweeper

school bus